# From Cross Hill

# From Cross Hill
Views of My Cuba

Richard M. Grove

*Third Edition*

**Published by**
**Hidden Brook Press**
writers@hiddenbrookpress.com
www.hiddenbrookpress.com

Copyright © 2011 Richard Grove
Second Edition 2009
First Edition 2008

No part of this book may be reproduced except by a reviewer who may quote brief passages in a review. The use of any part of this publication reproduced, transmitted in any form or by any means, electronic, mechanical, photocopied, recorded or otherwise stored in a retrieval system without prior written consent of the publisher is an infringement of copyright law.

From Cross Hill: Views of My Cuba
by Richard M. Grove

Cover Photograph – Richard M. Grove
Cover Design – Richard M. Grove
Layout and Design – Richard M. Grove

Typeset in Georgian

Printed and bound in USA

Library and Archives Canada Cataloguing in Publication

Grove, Richard M. (Richard Marvin), 1953-
　From Cross Hill : views of my Cuba / Richard M. Grove. -- 3rd ed.

ISBN 978-1-897475-71-3
1. Grove, Richard M. (Richard Marvin), 1953- --Travel--Cuba. 2. Grove, Richard M. (Richard Marvin), 1953- --Correspondence.  3. Cuba--Description and travel. 4. Cuba--Poetry.  I. Title.

PS8563.R75F76 2011　　　C818'.5409　　　C2011-902966-9

Dedicated to Martha and Rubén

and always
my darling wife Kim.
Life's journey would be so dull
without you.

# Contents

– Letters Home – *p. 1 – 36*

List of Poems:
- My Room – *p. 5*
- Blown By the Breeze of Hope – *p. 6*
- The Phantom Hand – *p. 12*
- Birds of Different Varieties – *p.*
- Untethered Demise – *p. 24*
- *Haiku* – *p. 25*
- From the Top of Cross Hill – *p. 26*
- The Diaz Garden – *p. 33*
- Complaints about Cuba – *p. 37*
- Haikuesk – *p. 38*
- This Place Called Now – *p. 53*
- Without a Word – *p. 57*
- In a Wave of Black They Shattered – *p. 58*
- Cuban Winter Rain – *p. 59*
- Haikuesk – *p. 59*
- The Sucking Waves – *p. 60*
- Makeshift Curlers – *p. 61*

List of Prose:

- Blue Cattle Green Cattle – *p. 29*
- Being in the Garden – *p. 37*
- Compañeros – *p. 39*
- The Frozen Bus Ride From Havana 2006 – *p. 42*

- Translation Notes – *p. 62*
- Mi Casa – *p. 52*
- Bio Note – *p. 64*

# Letters Home

### Holguín, Cuba, March 28 —April 4, 2008

# Letter #1

*See Author and Translation Notes at end.*

### Friday, March 28

*Mi amour, mis hermanos y hermana:*

I miss you all, all ready. I am in tears as I write; tears of joy that I am hear with my long missed family – Manuel, Adonay and Pablo, tears of gratitude that I am in a wonderful, safe, new amigo's casa particular – Martha and Rubén are so loving and warm, tears of sadness that I had to leave paradise to be in paraiso, tears of sorrow because you are not here to share this warm breeze with me.

Everything is *perfecto*, nothing – absolutely nothing could be better.

I walked from the wings of steel to my – unlocked luggage – to find it untouched – thank you divine Principle. The lock of Love carried it off of the plane to a waiting cab. By bicycle – soon to be Manuel's – is still packed in its slightly punctured box. I will re-assemble it now and spin my Canadian wheels over Cuban streets to find my calm adventure for the week.

My room is *fantástico*. It has four large louvered windows that let in lots of light when open but can be closed to keep the morning light out. The windows look out to a garden of peace and tranquillity. Inside there are four glass windows that close to shut out the sounds of the night and the early morning rooster. Through swaying green I hear some chickens clucking, a neighbours pig squealing at scraps tossed. A dog, barking at birds next door perks my attention from time to time. This is the Holguín that I have always known – children playing in the streets, the clip clop of horse drawn carts moving people, hay, plantain; moving everything that needs to be moved. Motor cycles zip past smoke belching trucks to meet destiny face on with optimism. Mi casa is not on a main road so is much more quiet than I have had in the past.

## My Room

has an air conditioner,
a requirement of mine,
that pumps the cool breeze of guilt
for at least part of the night.

It also has a fan that blows
the rest of the time
over my un-acclimatized,
Canadian, pampered body.
Cooling my inflated sense of entitlement

My fear that you might have yet a last spring snow storm at our Presqu'ile, almost island, home is at least consoled by the fact that you could have come with me – all or any of you. Don't worry, I am getting over the guilt of being here and turning on the a/c. We will see if I have the air conditioner on for more hours in nights to come. Will my guilt of using electricity cave to my need for pampered comfort or will my sense of entitlement cave to my planet saving conscience. As the early afternoon heats to 28°c I can pretty much guarantee how long my a/c will be on tonight.

How can I make this my winter home. Martha and Rubén have a phone line and an internet connection. Hmm is it possible to run Hidden Brook Press from the comfort of this casa paradise? The wheels of imagination are turning. How much will I have to pay every year to make this the winter hub of HBP and the CCLA. An internet connection may make my fantasy come true. I will have to pick the right moment to talk to Martha about the price attached to a long stay with email and the net.

You will be welcome to visit me any time you like. I can show you the Cuba that you will not see if you spend your only time on a resort groomed beach. Hmm. You come for a week to a resort in Guardalavaca and I will visit you there for a swim in the ocean and then you can come and stay with me at *mi casa particular* here in Holguín. Hmm the plan is unfolding. I'll put it out to the universe and see if it unfolds or folds in the shape of a kite or an envelope. I may have a painted picture in my mind but the paint on the canvas is still wet and I am willing to have it be, at least a slightly different picture. What ever the picture I am confident it will always be a beautiful one. If you know of anyone that would like to rent our Presqu'ile home for next winter they can have it. I will be on the next jet to Cuba.

By the way talking about getting to know Cuba I was talking to a woman on the plane down to Cuba that said she has been to Cuba 66 times. Every time to the same resort and as often as possible to the same room. She has never been off of the resort or learned a single word of Spanish. Here and her husband get joining rooms – one needs the extra bed to lay out your cloths you know.

* * *

Here is a poem that sprang to life in the millisecond that I saw a beautiful lemon yellow butterfly fly across the highway on my way to Martha and Rubén's *casa* from the airport.

## Blown by the Breeze of Hope
*for Martha and Rubén – March 28, 2008*

Sweet lemon butterfly of protest
pierces pollution
weaving treacherous belching trucks
to safety of paraiso.
Royal palms sway, resolute
in political climate
of impending change.

The slight, ever so slight breeze
of looming capitalism, fanned
by hope's false promise
flaps Cuba's red white and blue.

Our beautiful lemon butterfly
perches suckling at the blossom
of now, the nectar of content.

\* \* \*

I have to remind myself not to be fooled by my
false notions of prosperity. Much is needed by just

about everyone that one runs into in Cuba. Manuel and Adonay need much if you compare their needs and wants to ours.

Their cave, as Manuel calls it,
concrete bunker as I see it,
is filled with love,
filled with hope,
brimming with passion and warmth.
A new refrigerator stands with pride
on fates expectation of – all needs will be filled,
a new washer is poised to scrub with humility.

* * *

2:30pm – I have reassembled my bicycle and have taken it for a spin. I think I will have to tinker with the gears a bit but for now it is working fine.
Breaks are tight – no squeak,
handle bars are true
and I have mixed some Cuban air
with the Canadian air in the tires.
It is now a true hybrid

I told Manuel that I would go to his place in the late afternoon. I still have to buy some *agua con gas* and a treat for Pablo, oh and some juice for my sister Adonay – she loves fruit juice.

See you later, *hasta luago mi amigos*

Kim I love you and miss you. You should have come with me!!!! Just kidding *mi amour*. Get your book finished and I will publish it when I get home.

xxxooo
Tai


### Sunday, March 30th

Yesterday I had a wonderful time with my Cuban family, Manuel, Adonay and Pablo. We sat and talked and played and played for many hours. The magic trick of making a string disappear has universal appeal for a four year old. From one palm to the other it could never be found by Pablo.

In the afternoon Manuel and I went for a walk to the government store to buy their food rations. I was under the false impression that Cubans received a free ration of some food items. But this is not true. They purchase the items that are listed in their ration book with Cuban pesos which is far less than the regular market rate. Aside from food such as buns, milk, rice, beans etc. they also purchase some soap and toothpaste, kerosene for cooking fuel and soy oil for cooking, Their ration book that tells how many people there are in the family and their general age will prescribe how much food they are allowed to buy at that subsidy price. Everything is purchased with Cuban (People's) pesos not Cuban Convertible pesos (CUC). To give you an idea of the value of the different pesos. One CUC will purchase 25 People's Pesos. One CUC will purchase one USA dollar.

For a family of 5 one will spend about 50 pesos for all of the rations for one month – about 10 pesos per person. A professional doctor or professor will be paid 30 pesos a month. With the ration book rice is 24 centavos per pound, sugar is 10 centavos per pound. Don't forget that price is in People's Pesos 25 to 1. When one runs out of rice, or any other ration, one will have to buy that product on the open market for 10 or maybe 20 times the price. When times are lean one can only hope to make the rations last for the month.

I was in the department store buying my drink of choice – agua con gas – sparkling water – $1.15 CUC per 1 litre bottle. I have found a cheaper place that is on the way to Manuel's for 0.80. If you are not careful you can pay $2.00. I was also buying juice for my juice loving sister Adonay and found a freezer full of upside down ladies diving for meat. I won't go into detail about the colour of all of their panties. :-)

From moment to moment
a friendly rummaging woman would surface
with a large frozen block of meat,
looks of satisfaction whelmed over faces.
Heavy rattling clangs echo
from cart or wire basket.

As soon as I dared make my approach
this grande hombre was upside down
bum sticking in the air.
Moments later frozen fingers
like a deep sea diver I return to the surface
with prize of frozen, sunken treasure.
I turned to a lady and asked,
"*Lo siento, mi Español es limitado* –
I am sorry, my Spanish is limited –
What type of meat is this, *por favor*?"
"*Si, si* it is meat." she turns and disappears.
Another attempt – "*Lo siento señorita
mi Español es limitado*,
what kind of meat is this, *por favor*?"
The answer was a scowl
followed by a hasty retreat
into the anonymity of the bustling crowd.
Maybe she thought I was calling her
a hunk of meat – *Lo siento señorita*.

Upon presenting my treasure to my hostess – mi hermana – Adonay. I discovered it was liver. The largest hunk of liver that I had ever seen. We will be having fried liver and onions soon for dinner. I am not convinced that Adonay is particularly delighted with the prospect.

\* \* \*

With the desire to feel safe in the Cuban open air concept homes the occupants most often erect iron bars on their windows and around their open air dining and living rooms. Iron bars on windows does not sound all that attractive but painted white with fancy bent iron work they can actually be quite attractive. While this does make for a secure sense of harmony in one's life it also restricts movement between neighbours.


## The Phantom Hand
*for Adanay and her forever smile*

Water glugges
from bottle to pot
through floor to ceiling
chain link fence
smiles of gratitude are exchanged
for smiles of – you are welcome.

Beans are boiled in neighbours agua.
Less mineral salts or something the myth says
makes for better beans.

The phantom hand of camaraderie
also appears in Adonay's kitchen
from time to time.
Milk, cheese, slices of meat
pass in and out through iron bars.
The joy of sharing a window
between two kitchens
has its advantages.

* * *

While Martha is on email I will see if I can send this from her computer. I am reluctant to impose on her as she always looks so busy running the affairs of the house. I am on my way to Manuel's soon so will finish writing later. Manuel has email access at the university and will send emails for me any time.

Esperando verle.

Tai xxxooo

# Letter #2

My Dear Kimber:

My trip has mostly been wonderfully calm and wonderfully uneventful. Mornings and early afternoons at *mi casa particular* writing and editing with late afternoons and evenings at Manuel's visiting. I often return home and write for another hour or more before I go to sleep.

I have gotten to know Pablo better again – he is a wonderfully energetic, expressive boy – not timid in any way. He is affectionate towards me and seams to remember my visit from two years ago. I have spent time with Adonay as a sister – she is a wonderfully affectionate person – I do love her more as time passes. Manuel and I have spent much time simply "hanging out", talking about the CCLA, writing as well as talking about some internal Cuban life and politics – it is impossible to separate the two. We have spent some time editing some of his "Tales for Pablo" that I will publish one day.

I hope to get to The Hill of the Cross sometime soon and soak in some Cuban landscape inspiration. Cross Hill as it is otherwise known is a small mountain that has a view of the entire cithy of Holguín and beyond. I have been to the top a few times in other years, in fact I have done a series of paintings from there called "From Cross Hill".

**Tuesday, April 1**

Kim, you remember the tire hand-pump that you dug up from the basement so I could take it with me for my bike. It worked for only a few strokes and then it blew no air. Now I remember that it did not work and had long been designated for landfill. Well the same genius of need being the mother of invention also translates as need being the mother of repair. In true Cuban fashion I took it apart, monkeyed with a flange on the inside, put it back together, first the wrong way, then correctly and it works fine. It does not have enough power to fill a tire all he way but I did ride for a couple of days until I found a gas station with an air pump. Their air is still free here.

Hi Doogla, mi hermano – I have had a wonderfully productive time here. I finished a final edit on my *Psycho Babble and the Consternations of Life.* I will give it to you for a final read when I get back. It is wonderful to have finally finished it and even better still it is cool that I finished it while in Cuba. While here I have also written a preface that I hope you like. I look forward to seeing it published by your imprint. It is much better than the first ms I presented to you for editing. I am planning a trip up Cross Hill. I wish you were coming with me. There is a poem for you up there – I am sure more than one.

Manuel and I have been talking about plans to bring a literary group to Holguín and make it much more writing oriented than the Havana reading tour that we have done twice. I see ten of us sitting here in Martha and Rubén's back garden workshoping every morning during and after breakfast. I see finished books coming out of the experience. We are thinking about a day trip to Manuel's father's farm. A day trip to the city of Banes and maybe a day trip to the seaside historical city of Gibara. I will fill you in more later.

\* \* \*

I love my long drawn out breakfasts in the open air dinning room that faces the brick walled back garden.

birds of different varieties hover
hopping and chirping at my feet,
a rooster is still crowing, off in the distance,
a pitcher of orgastic orange juice perspires,
ringing the white table cloth,
a brimming plate of papaya orbited
by pale chunks of dripping pineapple,
a feast in its own right
there is a morning dove cooing
her song of content,
four buns, I eat two and save two for lunch
with my peanut butter,

two eggs broken and fried flat
with a thick slice of fried ham,
I have learned to discreetly
dab the excess grease off
at the risk of offending my host,
chunks of white cheese fill a saucer,
I eat it with the pineapple.
All of this food served with a pot of tea – the tea that Kim so kindly reminded me to bring – as the coffee, which I love, is not decafe – they have not heard of such a thing – has a deleterious affect on my body. I am looking forward to a decaf Star Bucks as soon as I get home. Sarah where are you when I need you? Dare I import my own decaf next trip?

With my writing I manage to stretch my breakfast well into the afternoon. Here I am at 1:40 and I still have a banana – oh so sweet – and some orange juice left.

I do not have to stretch my imagination to guess
how Hemingway must have lived.
Palm frawns bowing to the mango trees,
shading the ferns and vines that climb

the brick wall that is the home
to those little lizard type creatures,
are they called gingkos?
that dart to their next
motionless pose of safety.

I usually skip lunch as this breakfast carries me to dinner at Manuel's place every night.

* * *

Yesterday I took a ride on my bike with the intention of circumnavigating the street where I am staying. On my return to *mi casa* I keep having to first find the city square with the church and the post office and then finding my way the four blocks from there. Never have I managed to just come straight here, day or night.

Part of the difficulty is that the streets are all one way, here in this part of the city. It is a common thing that even the residential streets are one way. Well I went out and turned right. Two blocks and

turned right, another two blocks and turned right, another two and turned right. Yes eventually I got lost and had to find my way down to the square with the church and come four blocks to find home. Last night I was determined not to overshoot my mark. I turned confidently towards *mi casa particular* and arrived directly at the square with the church. How did I manage that? I have no idea. I am sure that the Cubans watching me must laugh out loud andthought I was loco.
Every street looks so much the same
low rise pastel green, blue or white houses
painted grates on each window
sometimes ornate
often painted white.
Imagine yourself trying to find your way
in the thick of modern suburbia
where all of the houses, too you, look the same
you turn the corner and find another palm tree
another rusty stop sign
another mango tree
another giant split leaf philodendrun
another dog that was maybe the same dog
but moved to another street.

Thank heavens for Cross Hill
and its radio tower lit.
They are my high night time landmarks
that send me home.

\* \* \*

Oh very nice a morning dove just flapped down from the stone wall into the garden. It is the distant cousin of our morning dove at home in Presqu'ile. They are one race without borders. They do not recognize or care that I am Canadian. She struts her head forward and coos at me with regard for how close she has inadvertently landed. "How is your day *mi amigo*? Are you going to sit there all day and flap your fingers or are you going to go out and see what the day has to offer?" She struts her head at me again and says, "If Kim were with you you would be out there by now."

Well it is 1:20 pm now and it is kind of hot so I think I will have a shower and a snooze – just a short one to refresh and take the long way around to Manuel's place.

I just talked to Wency. I am going to see him in the main square tonight – Tuesday – he says hi.

TTYS
Tai – xxoo

## Letter #3

Dear Kimber:

I hope you are saying hi to family and friends for me – tell them that I don't miss them one little bit!!!!!!!!!  :-)

I am having such a great time. Hours of writing in the mornings and then some review / editing in the evening before I go to bed. For some reason I don't feel very inspired poetically but I finished editing my collection of short stories and have written a 700 word preface for the book today.

I went up to Cross Hill today. The word "hill" is a bit of a misnomer. It is a MINI mountain. First you have to walk or in my case bicycle up hill to where the stairs start. It is a workout just getting to the starting place where the hill officially starts. Then you have to walk up 30 or 40 stairs just to get to the platform where the stairs start and then you have to walk up the almost 500 stairs to the top. I have walked up three or four other times other years but obviously it had been long enough ago that I had forgotten just how steep and long it is. I imagine that I am one of the very few that have ever walked up with a bicycle over their shoulder. Yes people were looking at me like I was *loco*. Every 50 steps I stopped for a rest before moving on. I did not want to over do it. It is not every day that I climb 500 steps. On the way up I was watching a child's kite. First I was under it, then at eye level and then well above it looking down.

**Untethered Demise**

A child's kite the size of a platter
maybe smaller, folded
from paper bag
with the pride of perfection
over twigs, launched
with scrap paper tail it soars
without boundaries, though tethered
it will fly as far as it's master's
string will allow. Untethered
it will dive to its demise.
Too short a string it will flounder
too long it will list and risk its failure.
Perfect tension it will flutter in harmony
for ever.

speck of black
in deep sky
vulture hovers

\* \* \*

over Cross Hill
vulture stands motionless
on stiff wind

The view at the top is wonderful. Cross Hill is at the top of a peek so you can see for many miles in every direction. You can see the ocean on a clear day. Kites, hawks, vultures, pigeons are all sailing the updrafts from the city. As you can imagine it is rather windy up there.

**From the Top of Cross Hill**

From the top of Cross Hill you look down
upon cloud's shadows cast
that roam the hills and flicker
rusted rooftops glance.

From the top of Cross Hill you look down
upon the black backs of gliding vultures
balancing wind swept soar
in constant death scoping vigil.

From the top of Cross Hill you look down
to poverty's bunkers dug
into earth's red crust where pride lives
in a new pair of Nikes traded for a smile.

From the top of Cross Hill you look down
to pigeon's gorgeous glide in
aerodynamic wing whips
flying tip to tip formations of joy.

From the top of Cross Hill you look down
to the sprawl of people zig zagging
their way from one form of busyness
that any major city, anywhere, is tired of being.

What else did I get up to today. I had dinner with Manuel and Adonay again. They are so generous with their hospitality. I saw some meat in a freezer again today and almost bought some but I knew they had little or no room in their fridge or freezer so I resisted. I left their place early today to meet up with Wency at 7:30 pm.

I dashed off a little bit late and met him in the main square. We talked for a long time and then he bought us both some ice cream that we ate in the park. He is a generous guy. I have been invited to have dinner at his home on Thursday night. I have invited him to dinner at Manuel's on Wednesday. Oh my goodness I am starting to run out off days. I wonder if I can extend my ticket – just kidding. I miss you and will come home on the prescribed ticket day.

And wouldn't you know it Wency knows Martha from the university though he had not met Rubén before. I met Martha and Rubén's daughter Keyla and her husband, hmm I met him the other day and can't think of his name – a very nice couple, friendly and easy to get along with. They have a gorgeous baby girl - Kamila. I met their son Maykel the other day also. Such a very nice family.

\* \* \*

Kimber: I was cleaning up files from the laptop this morning so I could make room to do a defrag and came upon this poem, email and short story that I sent you just over two years ago.

> On wings of steel
> will I be carried
> back to you
> from whence
> we only shared the moon.

**Friday, March 7th, 2006**

Today I packed up and left my casa particular at Deisy's and came to Gibara, a small sea port about 20 minute taxi away - $18

I had to stay in one casa particular and Manuel, Adonay and Pablo had to stay in another because they are Cuban. My political / cultural feathers are being ruffled. :-) but I am staying quiet and safe – don't you worry.

## Blue Cattle Green Cattle

No, No señor the blue cattle no stay with the green cattle at night. The blue cattle must sleep here and the green cattle must sleep there señor. Si, si señor, Mañana mañana. Tomorrow the green cattle and the blue cattle can get together and see each other again but they should never be together for certain things and never in the same pen overnight, señior. Next week some of the blue cattle will leave and some new blue cattle will come. No, no señior the green cattle never leave, only the blue cattle can come and go. Sometimes we let the green cattle leave but only on a short leash. We learned that if we give them a long leash the leash might break and they will not find their way back. It is for there own good senior. They have everything they need here and nothing will hurt them. Si, si señior they are happy here, we tell them that they are happy here and they don't want to leave if we keep the fence strong and high. We tell them that they love their home and they do. Only if a blue cow tempts them do they ever really want to leave.

Manuel liked my little metaphoric story. The metaphor is soooo obscure do you think that any one will get the point :-) Like much of my writing on Cuba I am sure it will not get published.

Manuel was booked into a nice but low grade casa particular but because Adonay forgot her identification cards for here and Pablo they would not let them stay. A green cattle without id is no cattle at all. So here we were in Gebara for a holiday weekend and they had no place to stay. Well Manuel talked the guy who organized their rooms for them into letting them stay at his house as a friend – paying under the table. I have to tell you about that in person. This place used to be a registered casa particular but was so run down that the Cuban government took away his license. Remind me to tell you about the squaller conditions. Manuel, Adonay and Pablo had to stay there and on top of that I had to hang out there with them because they were not allowed to come to my casa particular – no Cubans were allowed even to visit.

We just got back from a walk to the ocean and the

full moon was shining as big as a plate behind a palm tree. I wish you were here to see it.

I am in my casa with the a/c on getting ready for bed. We did go swimming today but I hope we will find a better beach so I can actually swim instead of paddle.

※ ※ ※

So that was part of my adventure two years ago. Yesterday Wency came in to my casa particular for a short visit. I don't know if he was officially permitted or if they were just tolerant because Martha new Wency from the university. I remember that Deisy two years ago used to make Wency register if he stayed for more than 3 – 4 minutes. Deisy was not happy to let me have visitors. Manuel spent a few hours here with me working yesterday. Again I don't know if Martha was just tolerant because Manuel is friends with Manuel or if the rules have become more relaxed.

\* \* \*

I have commented on the patio garden here. It makes the visit so pleasant. I was asking Rubén about the name of a plant that he has growing in a few places. It is called – Malango de Jordan.

It has a huge beautiful purple-green leaf. In some ways the patio is not very special because on three sides it has a patchwork of old bricks with some not very careful concrete patches. The floor of the garden is rough patched concrete BUT the magic of the place is the love and care that fills the place. Rubén and Martha have created magic where only concrete and bricks once were. Plants fill every corner in rusty old dented pots. Many variety of plants are hanging on or climbing up the 6 foot brick wall. It is a wonderful place to read, visit or work. The birds are back; Rubén tossed some rice down. There are three morning doves a few, sparrows and a few other birds that I don't recognize that come and go. I do hope we can organize a CCLA writers workshop here.

## The Diaz Garden
*for Rubén and Martha*

    In the Diaz garden there is a magical plant
    with purple green heart shaped leaves
    with in days the piercing purple spear
    penetrated into life, emerged
    unfolded into a splendid
    three foot tall leaf of pride.

If you tried to pull at the leaf before it is ready to open, in time, in natures time you would only harm the perfect leaf that will emerge. I was thinking about this in relation to Cuba. It needs to emerge slowly over time. Just because Fidel has stepped down it does not mean that the new leaders should brutally tear at the country and make it emerge into its new stage prematurely. It is time for change but the country will be torn apart if reform happens too soon, too fast. Fidel himself knows that change has to happen. In his wisdom he put his brother in charge who has already made some small growing changes that will grow into the beautiful leaf that it should be. From this beautiful plant will grow a beautiful leaf.

# Letter #4

My dear Kimber:

My flight leaves Holguín at 10:10 am. and arrives in Toronto at 15:00 – flight # 5031

The ticket person at the Toronto airport put the baggage stickers over my departure time so today I was figuring out when I have to leave. I was thinking departing 15:00 = 3pm oh man am I glad I double checked. I will be with you by 3:30 or 4.

see you soon
xxxooo

## Wednesday, April 2

Hola mi amour,

Here we are in April 2nd

I will try to paste a message from my memory card to this message on Manuel's computer. it is not all that complicated if it were not for be being at a Spanish computer.
I just got back from climbing Cross Hill. Almost 500 steps to the top carrying my bike. The steps are organized in sets of 25 with a small platform that usually has a bench. I did 2 sets of 25 each time before resting. 50 steps at a time eventually got me to the top. This grandi hombre is loco carrying his bike to the top of the mountain. Then I rode my bike down the back side of the mountain into poverty. I am sad to say that Holguín has such a slum. I don't mind seeing grass huts and cactus fences. It is just life from a different era but I do hate to see the stinking , dirty, squalor that some people live in. Slum is hardly the right word for how they live on the back side of the mountain though I am reminded that in the slums of Mexico they live in cardboard boxes in their slums.

I am here at Manuel's for dinner again so I should leave you now and visit with them. I will be seeing Wency at 7:30pm. Say hi to everyone for me

Hugs from Holguín

tai

xxxxoooo

Remind me to buy some picnic table cloth clips and give them to Martha the next time that I come. Martha and Rubén provide a wonderful large table in the outdoor dining room for eating. This is where I do much of my computer work but the table cloths are forever blowing up. These picnic table clips will solve the problem for them.

\* \* \*

## Complaints about Cuba

The roosters crow too early here
The nights are too long
The days are too short,
in fact there are too few many days
in a week while in Cuba
though smiles are wide
and friendships grow deep.

\* \* \*

## Being In the Garden

You are now sitting with me in the back garden of Martha and Rubén's Holguín paradise. Lush, plants whisper a poem of green to you as you settle into a comfortable chair. Your feet are planted on the still cool concrete floor, your bare legs are stretched out in the morning sun that leaks in past the swaying palms and penetrates to your core warming your chest and arms, you slowly sink further into your chair and lose your sense of being anywhere. All you know is this moment, there is nothing else. All of your worries, wants, needs disappear into nothingness. From one moment to another you are not even conscious of our body. Your muscles in your shoulders, in your neck slowly begin to relax, melt into hot wax, your arms slowly, gently fall to your side. Your breathing starts to slow one breath at a time. Your chest slowly rises and falls. The sun has crept up past your chest to your face, a calm smile slowly whelms over you until your entire body begins to smile. A morning dove flutters into the garden and lands at your feet. Your smile draws her into your peaceful space, she coos back at you. You float into the air out of your chair, the warmth of the sun over your body is cooled by a gentle breeze that carries a distant Cuban tune over the vine covered brick wall into this space called now. You leave everything but gratitude behind.

*For my friend Kate Marshall Flaherty*

\* \* \*

delicate butter-yellow trumpets
bob in noonday breeze

## Compañeros

Two compañeros, a pig and a chicken, sat under the reaching arms of an ancient guabba tree. "Which would you rather be a pig or a chicken?" said the chicken to the pig. "I never thought about it before. Which would you rather be?" sad the pig to the chicken.

They languored there for sometime in the glorious gold of the late afternoon leaning against the rather grand trunk, both with legs stretched out, one leg crossing the other. "There are many merits to each, mi compañera." said the pig to the chicken. "Many indeed." replied the chicken to the pig.

There was a gentle cool breeze that moved puffy white clouds into the depths of the rolling horizon. It was a calm and lazy afternoon. "Many merits indeed mi compañero. You get fed so much more food than me. Sometimes even table scraps and soon windfall apples, more than you can possibly eat. There are many merits for being a pig." said the chicken to the pig. "Many more merits indeed."

"Oh but you mi compañera are free to roam all day, I on the other hand am mostly cooped up in the rather crowded sty. I have to root my way under the gate just to get a breath of fresh air and a moments privacy. There are many more merits for being a chicken if you ask me." said the pig to the chicken.

"Well excuse me, señor, but while I do appreciate my freedom to roam you must appreciate the dangers of being a chicken, foxes, weasels and such, why just the other day we lost a compañera to a hawk. Ripped her to shreds poor thing. You on the other hand have the glorious luxury of snoozing after a wallow in the mud with no fear that anything other than a fly will tickle your nose." said the chicken to the pig.

"Well lets not get huffy about it, señora, chicken. There are more merits for being a chicken than a pig." said the pig to the chicken. "Many more merits indeed."

They sat there for the longest time pitching their arguments back and forth getting more and more heated as time went on. Chicken feed twice a day, clean straw to sleep in, never being chased by the dog, being able to roost in a tree. The list went on and on. Time slipped away until the sun was just peeking over the tree covered hills.

It was only with the clanging of the dinner bell, the farmer's wife calling the family to dinner that they stopped their arguing. "I wonder what they are having for supper tonight?" Said the chicken to the pig. "Hmmmm. I wonder mi compañera." said the pig to the chicken.

# The Frozen Bus Ride From Havana
## March, 2006

Time to leave Cuba's Capital; the frozen bus ride from havana, Oh what a painful, painful and painfully long, long bus ride from Havana to Holguín. First Manuel phoned and phoned and then phoned again, calling the Havana bus terminals to find out when the two different busses were leaving for Holguín. There are two different terminals. One is the fancy, Via Sol, tourist bus and the other is the, ASTRO, bus for the local Cubans. Both are for long distance travelling from city to city even from one end of the country to the other but the Via Sole one is the fancy one for tourists and costs more.

Neither of the companies answered their phones for days so finally, on this day of departure, we went out and hailed a cab to take us to the Via Sole terminal to book our tickets for what we presumed would be a 7pm departure time. For some reason we could not get a normal taxi so we reverted to a "parallel market" cab that stopped and offered us a ride. The driver, a slim, tanned Cuban with a brush cut, demanded $4, we offered $3, we should have offered $2. He readily accepted the $3 and we tore off in his dilapidated old Russian Lada that had no glass in the four side windows. The car was stripped of all interior decorative panels including the ceiling and was void of all fabric and rugs except for the front and the back lumpy seats. It was a quivering, all but derelict, hunk of steel in the shape of a car. Of course it had a makeshift radio that pumped out Latino music; it hung from its wires and swayed back and forth with the pulsing rhythm, the soul of Cuba, as we darted in and out of traffic. He wove through the streets with the skill of any Indi pro driver, skimming pedestrians, trucks and cars by inches. White knuckled I wondered if the hair on the back of my neck would ever lie down again. He dropped us at the terminal but around the corner out of sight of the Policía so he would not get caught transporting fares without a permit. I vote to never give him a permit.

As soon as we arrived in the terminal we discovered that the 7pm, and only bus of the day, was full. We ran out to see if the illegal cab was still there, thank heavens it wasn't. We hailed another cab and paid another $3 to have him whisk us over to the other terminal as fast as possible. Arriving there in a less harrowed state of mind, we dashed in and bought our tickets; the last two tickets for the day. Providence? You will soon see I wish we had missed the bus. We paid for the tickets $36 each; the other bus would have been $44. The saving of $16 is good on any day, in any country; or is it? We then dashed out to get yet another cab, another $3, back to Manuel's cousin's place to get our bags as this bus was leaving in 1½ hours. The trip to the Havana zoo will have to wait till the next visit.

Oh the wisdom of foresight – with the help of the woman cab driver we reserved a cab for 3:30pm to pick us up with our luggage – smart thinking I thought. 3:27pm we were down at the curb with a pile of luggage waiting, waiting and waiting but no 3:30pm cab came. How foolishly optimistic we were to think that a scheduled cab would actually show up.

I stayed with the luggage while Manuel dashed down the hill to the main street to hail a cab. NO CAB, NO CAB, NO CAB. Finally two nice Cuban guys walking past me and asked if I needed a taxi. One of them dashed to the other main street and hailed a taxi. I was loading our luggage within two minutes. Well now I have the luggage in the cab but no Manuel – he is still looking for a cab. We can't leave without Manuel so the driver backs the car down the long hill, against the flow of traffic, cars honking left and right, with me hanging out the window hollering for Manuel while the cab driver honked furiously as he cleared a path. Finally Manuel sees us, runs half way up the hill, gets in the car and it. . . just sits there engine grinding. We are now too heavy to drive up the steep hill. Horn honking, driver gesticulating we back the cab further to the bottom of the hill and take a running start in low gear to slowly, ever so slowly, chug to the top of the hill. This car was a true Rolls Canardly – rolls down the hill but canardly make it to the top. Well finally arrived at the terminal, paying another $3; we rush in to get in line for our bus with just a few minutes to spare.

In typical Cuban fashion we had to show our id, me my passports and Manuel his government identification papers, not just to buy the tickets but to make our way into the departure lounge, guarded by three security guards. Apparently, this step was only the bureaucratic method of keeping freeloaders from hanging around in the air conditioning of the departure lounge. Well perhaps it also employed three Cubans that might otherwise need a job – Castro boasts of his 100% employment rate. This figure might be disputed depending with whom you speak but at any rate I am sure glad I had my passport handy.

We dragged our luggage, squeezing in past the security guards and thronging crowds only to find that we should not have taken our luggage into the departure lounge but rather to the luggage check-in location on the other side of the terminal where we entered. Frustrated, in these last few minutes, Manuel dashes out past the three guards leaving me to mind the ample carry on bags that we were still burdened with. Upon returning he explained that he had to tip, or in Canadian terms, bribe, the luggage handler guy 50 pesos to take our overweight bags; a small price to pay considering it was a bribe to an official government employee. If we had thought about this "tipping" process earlier we would have ignored the 20kilo per bag and included our other large bag that we were going to try to squeak on as carry-on.

Now finally with our large over sized carry-on and other bags in tow we headed to board the bus. With protest I explained to Manuel that I was not going to get on the bus until I had seen our luggage safely stowed on board. BUT meanwhile unbeknownst to us because we had not boarded the bus yet, because we were running around with our luggage they had not counted our heads and were going to sell our seats right from under us. Never was there an announce-ment suggesting that, all should be boarded. This disastrous event was only diverted because the kind ticket sales person saw us and remembered which location we were going and ran across the terminal to tell the bus driver that we were the missing passengers and they could not sell our tickets. In hind sight I regret thanking him.

Well despite this seeming good fortune I was still not about to get on the bus without our luggage actually being sighted and placed on the bus. There it was standing in the cool dark shadows of the shipping room behind the "official" cardboard, hand written 'No Passo' sign. "Señor, my luggage is not on the bus yet, it is there." – "No, No señor, all of the luggages are on the bus." – "No, No señor, there is our luggage right there. I can see it in the dark right there." – "Oh, si señor those luggages are going too, don't you worry. Put your other big bag on with those señor. Jose, put these three in the Holguín section on the other side of the bus." Jose wheeled his cart out of sight, three bus shaking thuds indicated that our bags were safely stowed. Oh what a relief that our luggage was loaded and we were now, finally, boarding the bus. "Señor, I need your ticket and your passport, por favor."

After showing our id one more time we are now on the bus; oh my goodness it is literally a brand new bus. It smelled of new. Plastic covered everything including the seats, the magazines, the armrests, headrests – Everything. Everyone including me was thrilled with the grand newness, that is until they were settled in their seats for two and a half seconds. Well then the outcry started. "Oh my god these seats are so small. They were made for a little China man," the protest starts. "How am I going to go 700 kilometres sitting in this little padded can," they moaned aloud.

Pointing at me, a little Cuban woman says, "Look at him; he's a grande hombre, he isn't going to fit in these little seats." Well they did and they will again I am sure but as that lady said, I wouldn't and I didn't and I would never again try.

It was the most uncomfortable ride I had ever had or could ever imagine having. When the person in the seat in front of me reclined their seat it grazed my beard and landed on my chest. I could literally put my chin on the back of the seat and as for my knees, well that was nigh on impossible to fathom how even a "little China man" could possibly be comfortable for an hour let alone 12. Oh my god. What would be my saving grace? – a toilet pit – that's right there was a toilet room in the basement of the bus; that is right, the basement of the bus as I called it. There was this little space just big enough to stand in to open the door to the toilet that became my home for the next twelve hours. One had to step down three steps into this pit at almost ground level. Once you were in the pit you had to pivot around with out moving your feet so you could then point in the right direction of the toilet door. My new space was outside of the

– Baño – bathroom but it was a brand new baño. The Baño itself was so small that the door could not close with a "normal size" person inside. It was smaller than any aeroplane bathroom, an absolute joke. I could not have imagined using the Baño and in fact I did not. This bathroom pit entrance was to be my home for the next 12 hours. I learned to be grateful despite the pain, for the privilege of sitting on the little steps outside of this little basement bathroom foyer. I am so glad that only 2 people made me move from my relatively luxurious resting place.

Well aside from the cramped conditions I must tell you about the air conditioner. Yes it worked and it worked well, in fact too well. I can safely call my trip 12 hours of freezing hell. There was a very fancy digital readout panel at the front of the bus that told the time, I saw every 722.5 minutes of my 12 hour tick by. It also showed the outside temperature, 27oc by the way and the inside temperature that ranged from 14oc down to 8oc. It would be safe to say that the average temperature inside was 10oc the entire trip. It was totally freezing. I have been known to hyperbolize from time to time but this was truly 12 hours of freezing hell.

Visualize this – a bus load of Cubans that normally feel that 22oc is time to put on a jacket. Use your mind's eye and see them all hovered under blankets, shirts and sweaters. One half frozen woman had a pair of socks on her hands and a pair of underpants on her head. Everyone including myself had whatever article of clothing pulled up over their heads for virtually the entire trip. At one awkward moment someone farted and someone else yelled – at least it is hot. This intercourse including the flatulence took place in Spanish, by the way.

Saturday, March 11/ 06: We arrived in the cool calm of Holguín at 5am. We peeled ourselves from under whatever clothes and blankets we had and staggered to throbbing terra firma. It would be many hours before the ground and body would stop pulsing the rhythm of that Asian bus "built for a little China man". We dragged our luggage from under the bus – we knew exactly where it was and piled it into a horse-drawn carriage that would take me to my casa particular and Manuel to his home to see his wife Adonay and his almost 2-yr old son Pablo. Deisy greeted me with blurry eyed enthusiasm and showed me to my room. She reminded me where the bathroom was, the light switches and how to turn on the air conditioner. A shiver rushed through my bones as I turned off the light and fell into bed. I slept 4 hours and woke with the tremors of that shocking bus ride still frozen into memory.

## This Place Called Now

February 2009

Estimado Hermano / Dear Brother:
(*a letter poem from one brother to another*)

Beautiful here mi hermano, sunny and fresh,
a little windy,
the fields, they are filled
by the colourful, little flowers
of late Cuban winter.
This morning your sister, singing
in happiness.

>*Good afternoon my brother.*
>*I see you were on line at the moment*
>    *I was getting email.*
>*This is the closest that I feel to you when*
>    *our electrons cross paths and our*
>    *email syntax fills the ether.*
>*Thank heaven for the miracles of melted*
>    *silicone and wires.*
>*At this moment, in my place of winter,*
>    *at my desk*

*I am looking out to a breathtaking half
    moon painted
on a rippleless blue canvas. Such a
    gorgeous day.
I know you are looking at the same
    moon.
The sun and the moon brings our
    desks closer my friend.
They bring us to this place called now.*

*I got your email today. Such a busy
    man you are with so many
    things to do in your life.
I am sure you will live to be 110
    because you will forget
    to stop and die.*

*I miss you and Cuba, mi hermano
the coffee, the rooster's crow
the snorting pig from beyond.
I miss the red earth – la tierra roja
the foundation for where
you sink your roots.*

*Today is only moderately cold -17oc*
*but the sun, the same sun that warms*
*you is filling my Presqu'ile home*
*bringing me*
*a little taste of Cuba spread*
*across my living room floor*
*honey spilled from the pot of longing.*

*I wish, I so very much wish, I could*
*be with you, my sister Adonay,*
*and Pablo for dinner tonight,*
*put my feet under your table*
*and join in our family time.*

*Hugs from beyond this time of place.*


For place is now, forever here
now this cool air over my island brings
aromas of your pine groves
the earth whirls east and I see
the frozen breath of my tall brother
in heavy coat walking by his frozen lake.

Now is a place to meet with Pablo
in need for tales to go to bed
his heavy eyes, his tiny voice
his rough nobility of innocence.
The earth will whirl, the wind will blow
the child he is now forever gone.

Love is timeless and is it's own place;
hermano mío, your now is here
forever here.

Manuel Velázquez León<br>
y Richard M. Grove

## Without a Word

When you came to me
it was just a little past noon
and still the rooster rose
above a distant clarinet
scaling up then down
        up then down
in practiced perfection.

I had intended
to sit in the Cuban sun
and read the wisdom of José Martí,
ponder his words and meditate
but the longing call
of my rooster friend
drew me to the top
of the stuccoed wall.
There in the shimmering green
of a Bioba tree
I was instantly,
without a word
with you and Martí.

## In a Wave of Black They Shattered

Twenty-five or maybe thirty toti
with unceremonious clatter
fluttered their way into the large tree
that sheltered the back yard
of our casa.
Like children descending
on a quiet school yard
they joyously invaded
our quiet breakfast
and then in a wave
of black they shattered
the brilliant blue sky
and departed.

## Cuban Winter Rain

Last night there was
a very gentle sparse rain
on our very dry meadows.
Today it is sunny and hot,
the aroma of dry grass
once again fills the air.
Whims of the tropics
in winter.

                                      Manuel Velázquez León
                                         y Richard M. Grove

## The Sucking Waves

The sea was filled
with rage last night.
Foaming, churning,
whipped to crashing crests.
Low led clouds
shed shafts of cold rain
careening to dancing beach
pitted deep.

Flung beyond surf line
blue swollen man-of-wars
laying in wait for foaming
burst to carry them back
on sucking waves.

Today calmed to placid blue
under dour pink.
Sacrificial lambs strewn
lifeless
poisonous purple tentacles dead
yet still poised
for unsuspecting
tourist victim's tread.

## Makeshift Curlers

A proud Cuban woman
weaves through
department store aisles,
necessities plunk into basket.
Cardboard toilet-paper rolls,
makeshift curlers,
furrow her black hair.


           Brilliant noonday sun
           strokes glorious palm
          You have never seen green
    until you have seen a Royal Palm
        glide against Cuban sky.

**Translation Notes:**

– Amigo / Amiga – Friend – male / female
– mi hermana  / mi hermana – my brother / my sister
– Casa particular – a private home – like a bed and breakfast
– paraiso – paradise
– hasta luago – til later
– mi – my
– mi amour – my love
– agua – water
– agua con gas – water with gas / soda water
– grande hombre – large man
– Lo siento, mi Español es limitado. – I am sorry, my Spanish is limited.
– por favor – please
– esperanto verle – looking forward to seeing you

**La casa de mis amigos**

This is the info for the casa particular (Villa Azul) where I stayed. I have no hesitation if recommending that you stay there. Let Rubén and Martha know that I recommended them to you.

Owners:
Rubén Díaz Leyva (Lawyer)
Martha Felipe Gamboa (Teacher)

Address:
Rastro # 35 e/ Agramonte y Garayalde, Holguín
Cuba.

Tel (53-24) 42 9603

Email: rubendl@enet.cu

http://www.villa-azul.com/index_eng.htm

**Richard M. Grove,** otherwise known by his friends as, Tai, is a man of the 7 Ps – Poet, Publisher, Painter, Potter, Photographer, Public speaker and even Person. Richard has been going to Cuba, once or twice a year for 12 or 15 years now. He is the president of the Canada Cuba Literary Alliance. Find the CCLA at: www.CanadaCubaLiteraryAlliance.org.

He takes groups of Canadian authors to Cuba on reading and writing tours and then publishes their work. He has given readings interviews and talks on publishing and writing around the world including Germany, New Zealand and Cuba. Find out who the real man is at: http:www.poetsencyclopedia.com/richardgrove.shtml

He lives in Presqu'ile Provincial Park with, his freelance writer wife, Kim. At their Presqu'ile home they rent cottages and run a writers / artist retreat.

You can find them at 109 Bayshore Road, RR#4 Brighton, Ontario, Canada, K0K 1H0
or writers@HiddenBrookPress.com.
www.HiddenBrookPress.com

# CCLA

Would you like to come on our annual CCLA literary trip to Cuba?

Workshops
Daytrips,
Readings,
Publishing ops
and a holiday in the sun.

Ask a CCLA Ambassador in your area.
*www.CanadaCubaLiteraryAlliance.org*